Clarinet / Klarinette / Clarinette / 1

My FIRST Melodies

34 children's tunes · 34 chansons enfantines
34 Kinderlieder · 34 kinderliedjes

 *de haske*®

edited by
Michiel Oldenkamp

Order number: DHP 1063997-400

My First Melodies
edited by Michiel Oldenkamp
Clarinet

ISBN 978-90-431-2479-6
ISBN 90-431-2479-6
NUR 472

CD number: DHR 13-441-3
Midi-production: Peter van der Zwaag

My FIRST Melodies

Foreword

This is a collection of very easy, well-known children's tunes. You may not know all of them but you have probably learned some of them at school or in music lessons. Enjoy playing the tunes with the play-along CD: they'll sound really cool! The first tune is the easiest. As you go through the book the tunes gradually get more difficult, step by step, so you keep learning in an enjoyable way.

Have you never played along with a CD before?

1. First practise the tune without the CD. Do this as often as you need to play it well.
2. Listen to the play-along track and try to sing along while reading the notes. Do not play along yet.
3. Play the tune along with the CD.

Before the tune starts you will hear several taps. These taps help you to start playing at the same time as the CD.

Have fun!

Vorwort

Dies ist eine Sammlung von sehr einfachen, bekannten Kinderliedern. Du kennst sie vielleicht nicht alle. Einige sind dir aber sicherlich schon in der Schule oder im Instrumentalunterricht begegnet. Besonders viel Spaß macht das Spielen zur Mitspiel-CD – so klingt es richtig cool! Das erste Lied ist das einfachste. Im Laufe des Buches werden die Melodien allmählich – Schritt für Schritt – schwerer, so dass du spielend lernst.

Hast du noch nie zu einer CD gespielt?

1. Üb das Lied zunächst ohne die CD und zwar so oft, bis du es gut spielen kannst.
2. Hör dir die Begleitung an und versuch, mitzusingen und die Noten mitzulesen. Spiel jetzt noch nicht mit.
3. Spiel das Lied zur CD mit.

Vor dem Anfang eines Stückes hörst du ein paar Schläge. Diese Schläge helfen dir, gleichzeitig mit der CD einzusetzen.

Viel Spaß!

Avant-propos

My First Melodies est un recueil de célèbres chansons enfantines. Certaines d'entre elles vous sont familières, d'autres sont à découvrir. Toutes possèdent un accompagnement sur compact disc, frais et coloré, pour vous permettre de les interpréter avec beaucoup de plaisir. Les premières mélodies sont les plus faciles à jouer. Le niveau d'exigence augmente pas à pas. Ainsi, vous progresserez efficacement sans jamais perdre de vue l'essentiel : le plaisir du jeu.

Si vous n'avez pas l'habitude de jouer avec un compact disc, il vaut mieux procéder de la façon suivante :

1. Écoutez la version intégrale du morceau pour vous faire une première idée de la pièce.
2. Travaillez la pièce sans l'accompagnement jusqu'à parfaite maîtrise.
3. Écoutez la partie d'accompagnement (sans la partie solo) en effectuant une lecture de notes simultanée.

Les morceaux débutent avec une courte indication de pulsation (clicks de départ). Cela permet de bien sentir le tempo et d'avoir des repères pour démarrer de façon synchronisée avec le compact disc.

Amusez-vous bien !

Voorwoord

Dit is een verzameling van zeer eenvoudige en bekende kinderliedjes. Misschien ken je ze niet allemaal, maar je hebt er vast wel een aantal van geleerd op school of tijdens de muziekles. Speel ze lekker mee met de begeleidings-cd: dat klinkt gaaf! Het eerste liedje is het gemakkelijkst en verderop in het boek worden de liedjes stap voor stap een beetje lastiger. Zo leer je er steeds wat bij op een leuke manier.

Heb je nog nooit eerder met een cd meegespeeld? Houd dan de volgende werkwijze aan:

1. Oefen het liedje eerst zonder de cd. Doe dit zo vaak als nodig is om het goed te spelen.
2. Luister naar de begeleidingstrack en probeer mee te zingen terwijl je de noten meeleest.
   Speel nog niet mee.
3. Speel het liedje samen met de cd.

Voordat een liedje begint, hoor je een paar tikken, zodat je precies op tijd kunt beginnen met spelen – dit heet 'intikken'.

Veel plezier!

Contents · Inhalt · Sommaire · Inhoud

Track/Plage   Page/Seite/Blz.

= Accompaniment only / Begleitung (ohne Solostimme) /
Accompagnement (sans la partie solo) / Begeleiding

Stille, stille

Song of Silence
En silence
Stil, stil

Hänsel und Gretel

Hansel and Gretel
Hansel et Gretel
Hans en Grietje

4

Boer, daar ligt een kip in 't water

Chicken in the Water
Bauer, da liegt ein Huhn im Wasser
Une poule dans la mare

5

Hört ihr die Drescher

Listen to the Thresher
Les moissoneuses-batteuses
Luister naar de dorser

Heut' ist ein Fest

Party Time Today
Aujourd'hui c'est jour de fête
Het is feest vandaag

Daar was laatst een meisje loos

There Was Once a Clever Girl
Zur See einmal ein Mädchen fuhr
La petite fille malicieuse

Jack and Jill

Jack und Jill
Jack et Jill
Jan en Jansje

Slaap, kindje slaap

Sleep, Little One
Schlaf, Kindlein schlaf

Der Mond ist aufgegangen

The Moon Is Risen
La lune s'est levée
De maan is opgekomen

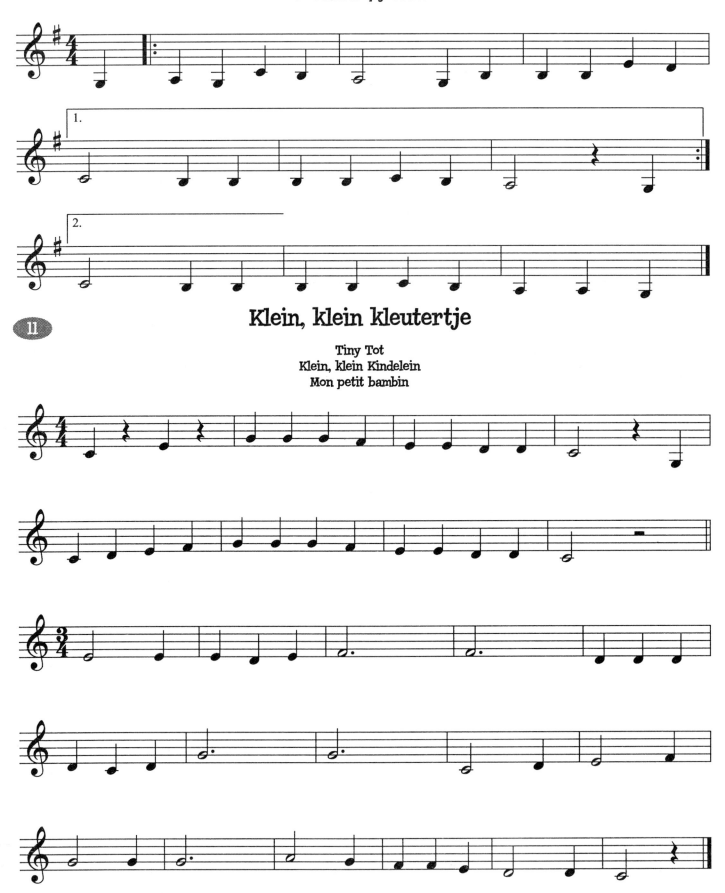

Klein, klein kleutertje

Tiny Tot
Klein, klein Kindelein
Mon petit bambin

12

Boer, wat zeg je van mijn kippen?

Chicken Stew
Meine Hühner sind die schönsten

Fine

D.C. al Fine

13

Oh Where, Oh Where Has My Little Dog Gone?

Ach wo, ach wo ist mein kleiner Hund hin?
Où est passé mon petit chien ?
Waar is mijn hondje heen gegaan?

Pop Goes the Weasel

Weg ist das Wiesel

Mevrouw van Roosendaal

Mrs. Malmesbury
Freifrau von Rosenthal
Madame Deshouches

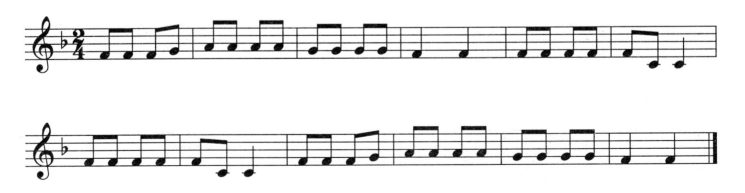

16

Hopp, hopp, hopp

Giddy-Up
Hop, hop, hop

17

Grün, grün, grün sind alle meine Kleider

Top to Toe in Green
Tout en vert
Van top tot teen in het groen

Elsje Fiederelsje

Rosie Twinkletosie
Elli Fiederelli
Angélique Micmacmique

Hot Cross Buns

Rosinenbrötchen
Briochettes aux raisins
Krentenbollen

14

Mäuschen, lass dich nicht erwischen

Little Mouse, Don't Let 'Em Catch You
Caline la souris maline
Muisje, laat je niet vangen

Taler, Taler, du musst wandern

Money Movers
Un sou neuf s'en va en promenade
Geld moet rollen

C-a-f-f-e-e

C-o-f-f-e-e
Pause-Café
K-o-f-f-i-e

Aram sam sam

Die Schneckenpost

24

Snail Mail
La poste-escargot
De slakkengang

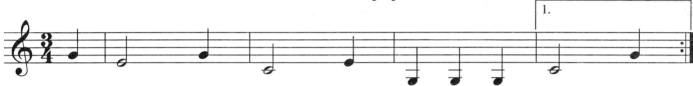

Dornröschen

25

Sleeping Beauty
La Belle au Bois Dormant
Doornroosje

Trarira, der Sommer, der ist da

Hooray, it's Summertime!
Voilà, l'été est là !
Hoera, de zomer is begonnen

26

Berend Botje

Billy Bobbin's Boat
Karlchen Kutter
Oh-hisse et Ho !

27

28

In meinem kleinen Apfel

My Little Apple

29

Ding Dong Bell

Ding, Dong, Glocke
Les cloches carillonnent
De klok slaat

The Skye Boat Song

Boot, fahr mich nach Skye

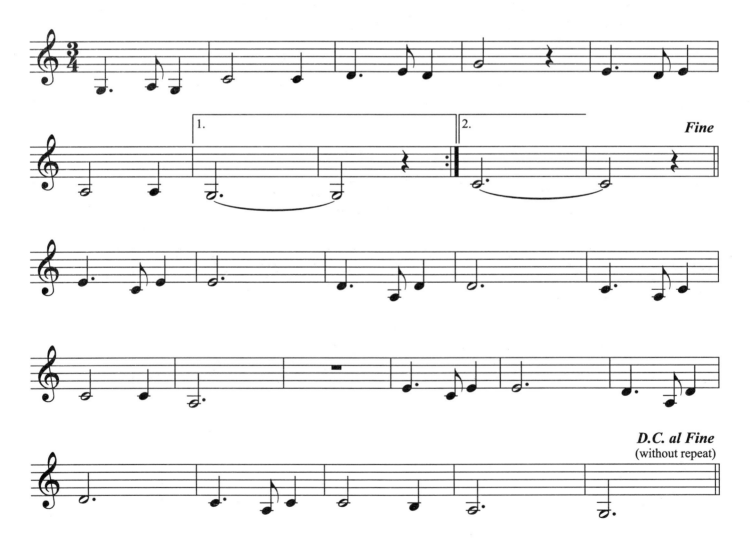

Kumbayah

31

Morning Has Broken

Lumière du matin

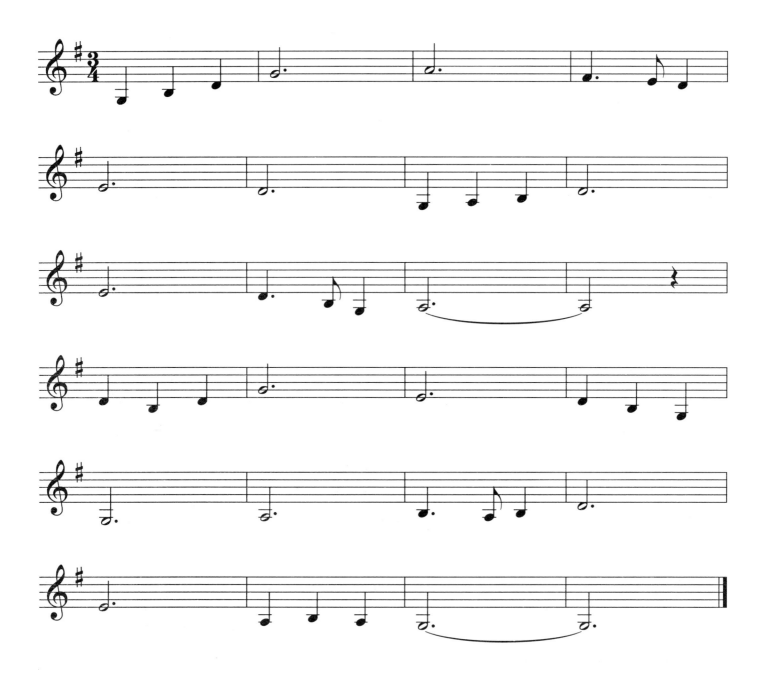

Alle Vögel sind schon da

Here Come the Birds
Le retour des oiseaux
Alle vogels zijn present

Laurentia

Sing a Song of Sixpence

Das Pfenniglied